I am
dragon

I am
dragon
how to unleash your fiery side

kirsten riddle

CICO BOOKS
LONDON NEW YORK

Published in 2018 by CICO Books
An imprint of Ryland Peters & Small Ltd
20–21 Jockey's Fields   341 E 116th St
London WC1R 4BW   New York, NY 10029

www.rylandpeters.com

10 9 8 7 6 5 4 3 2 1

Text © Kirsten Riddle 2018
For recipe text credits, see page 144.
Design and illustration © CICO Books 2018
For photography credits, see page 144.

A CIP catalog record for this book is
available from the Library of Congress
and the British Library.

ISBN: 978-1-78249-603-8

Printed in China

Editor: Marion Paull
Designer: Emily Breen
Illustrator: Trina Dalziel
(Artworks on pages 12–13 by Roger and
Linda Garland; artwork on page 41
by Paul Stradling)

Senior editor: Carmel Edmonds
Art director: Sally Powell
Production controller: Mai-Ling Collyer
Publishing manager: Penny Craig
Publisher: Cindy Richards

contents

introduction

My fascination with dragons started at a young age, thanks to the delightful tale of Puff the magic dragon who lived by the sea. He may be the stuff of fantasy and a cherished childhood memory, but he planted a seed in my mind—mystical creatures were out there and I could discover them. They were within my grasp in the form of stories, wonderful, compelling, and often heart-stopping narratives that would set my imagination on fire. While Puff is hardly the flame-throwing, demonic monster you might expect (he was green and slightly podgy, and had a kind heart), I was hooked.

The older I got, the more I began to unearth about these enthralling beings. Yes, there was the Western scary version, riveting and perilous, the terrifying fiend of so many stories and folk tales, but there was also the Eastern version. This dragon was an altogether different beast with a benevolent approach and a clever mind. A sacred sentinel endowed with grace and compassion, this dragon had the ability to bestow all manner of divine gifts upon us mere mortals. The legends revealed two sides of the same coin, opposing in their influence and yet equally important. This was intriguing and something that I had to learn more about.

As a storyteller, it's essential to know the core message of your tale, the heartbeat that breathes life into the narrative.

Dragons play an important role in myth and legend around the world, but why and how could they be so different? Could the disparity between East and West be part of the answer to the question and key to our captivation? Dragons, after all, offer us a balanced view of events—there is light and there is darkness, always two options, two ways of seeing and being. Symbols of strength and courage, they represent the innate power we have inside us and the potential to do great things. When we feel weak and vulnerable, dragons lift us up. They inspire us to keep going, to be better, and to reach for more. As they soar through the sky, leaving a fiery trail in their wake, they break through the thunder clouds, opening up

new opportunities and illustrating that with sheer determination and bravado you can make your way in the world. It doesn't matter what life throws at you, you have the ability to rise above it, to find inner strength, and to fly in the face of adversity. Perhaps this is why we have been fascinated with dragons for centuries, and why the myth lives on today. They offer us hope, and although they may at first appear supernatural, they prove that anything is possible. In a world where dragons exist, anyone can achieve their dreams.

As humans, we like to make sense of the world through stories. We give ourselves role models, physically and spiritually. Dragons may be the stuff of legend, but they epitomize so many admirable qualities and talents that we aspire to. Significant archetypes, they trigger our subconscious into action and help us access an inner well of personal power. It makes sense, then, that we can learn to work with this energy in order to manifest positive change. You can do this in your own unique way, and this book shows you how, whether you fancy learning about dragons from mythology, or losing yourself in popular fiction. You may find that gazing at them on the big screen sets your heart alight, or you could show your love in other ways by opting for a distinctive tattoo or a dragon-inspired hairstyle. Feeling magical? Turn your hand to some dragon-themed spells, or call on your own dragon guide for advice and protection.

This book is a treasure trove of all things dragon, your one-stop shop for inspiration. It will help you connect with the energy of this mythical creature. From starry dragons in the sky, to those peering from ornate tapestries or garden gates, every creature has its place and its use. So whether you want to get to grips with your inner dragon and show the rest of the world your mettle, or you see yourself as a potential dragon queen, you can find the answers you need, and a whole lot more, in these pages.

But be warned, dragons bring with them responsibility, too. These are not frivolous beings. When they act, it is with great courage and purpose; every choice is made for a reason. Dragons urge us to take responsibility for our actions, be in control of our destiny, and make the most of every day while honoring our true path.

With that in mind, there is only one thing left to say. Go forth and, in a serpentine fashion, plunder this tome, and remember …

Think bright, think glorious, think dragon!

PART 1

DRAGON

lore

Conjure up the image of a dragon. What do you see? For some, it's a huge fire-breathing monster, unforgiving in its hunger for human blood. For others, it's a more benevolent being, with gleaming scales and ocean-pool eyes, filled with mystery and wonder. The truth is, dragons are fluid. They can be all things to all people, changing in the blink of an eye and evolving over time. It's hard to pin them down, and that's the point! Dragon lore is an interwoven mix of legend and narrative. Delve deep and you may find the answers you seek, along with many more questions…

where do dragons come from?

No one knows exactly how the dragon myth developed, but scholars believe that it evolved independently around the world, and that it has its roots in ancient creatures. Mankind, influenced by the existence of a range of weird and wonderful animals, took inspiration from them to create the dragon, a beast that embodied many different characteristics. Some theorize that dinosaur fossils may have been the key, and it makes sense that if dinosaurs can exist, then something equally remarkable might have lived, or be living, among us.

For others, it was a specific creature that sparked the myth, whales being cited for their enormous bones. To the ancient mind, the discovery of such relics must have stirred a whole host of images and triggered some imaginative tales.

The Nile Crocodile is another contender. This huge creature often grew to around 18 feet (5.5 meters) long and could lift its upper torso from the ground in something called a "high walk," which must have looked very scary and possibly supernatural at the same time. For those with no scientific knowledge, this must have seemed like a living, breathing monster, so it's easy to see how the myth could have taken shape. Whatever their origins, dragons have become an enduring and iconic symbol, so the question is really "why do dragons exist?" rather than how they came about.

why do they exist?

Dragons fulfill a need. As humans, part of our survival instinct is that we fear the unknown, particularly if it comes in the shape and size of a fire-spilling dragon. Despite this, we are also entranced. The unknown captivates us, and dragons represent both sides of this. They're enchanting, magical creatures, and we don't quite know what they'll do next. These bewitching beasts have us at odds in our opinion of them, but that depends on where the dragon hails from.

European dragons tend to get a bad press. In the Middle Ages the word "dragon" was associated with war, and tales described them as horrific fire-breathing demons, wreaking havoc on the land and slaughtering innocents. Typically, stories suggested that the dragon needed some form of appeasement, usually the sacrifice of a young maiden, to quell its appetite for destruction. Even the Bible gives them a mention, although far from complimentary. The term "the Great Dragon" refers to Satan, and he is also called "that old serpent." This goes some way toward explaining our fear of these legendary beings. The name itself comes from the Greek *drakon*, meaning "dragon" or "serpent," and this is

DRAGON GUARDS

Whether from the East or West, the dragon's ability to guard is legendary. In Greek myth, Ladon is the dragon who protects the golden apples in the Garden of the Hesperides. This beast, thought to be the offspring of two sea deities, is there at the request of the goddess Hera, and he remains entwined around the tree, a fearsome sight with as many as a hundred heads. Eventually, Ladon met his doom at the hands of Hercules, by means of a poisoned arrow. Hera, aggrieved by his death, cast his image into the night sky, where he remains as the constellation Draco. While he might have seemed a scary monster in the tale, in reality this beautiful arrangement of stars in the northern sky is simply keeping a watchful eye on Earth. In China, the dragon is the ultimate symbol of protection and features in many temples and shrines, peering from ornate artistry to cast a discerning eye over those who visit. In Norse mythology, Fafnir is the dragon who lives high in a mountain cave, guarding an abundance of treasure from thieves and marauders.

thought to be derived from the Indo-European *derk*, which means "to see." Originally it meant "staring one," and it's thought that comparisons to snakes may have something to do with this, since they lack eyelids. In any case, dragons' eyes became a fearful and menacing sight.

While these mythical creatures are persecuted in the West, in the East it's a different story. In China dragons are associated with good fortune and success. They bring wealth, health, and a whole host of positive attributes, so much so that they are considered sacred. Divine in stature, these beautiful beings are friendly and enjoy helping humankind. Unlike Western dragons, they are associated with the element of water, in particular lakes, rivers, seas, and rain. They are a representation of nature and are seen as nurturing, bringing forth the changing seasons and encouraging new growth. While we might run from a towering dragon in the West, in the East their breath is known as *sheng chi*, the essence of all life. Since they are a symbol of infinite wisdom, it's no surprise that they're most closely associated with royalty. At the dawn of time the very first emperor, Fu Hsi, was thought to have the

tail of a dragon, and today China is known as a country descended from dragons.

How the dragon uses its power may differ around the world, but it is universally acknowledged as a symbol of strength. With so many varying narratives, it's easy to see how dragons have become a popular and prominent part of culture, representing choice and our ability to rise above a situation and emerge triumphant. Dragons give us a sense of balance, because they can be taken in so many different ways. Their deeds show us that we can use the fire in our bellies to change the world in a positive way. We can overcome negative impulses and evolve to become something truly magnificent, like this winged beauty.

A

DRAGON

NEVER FAILS IN HER

QUEST

FOR

SUCCESS

chinese dragons

An integral part of Chinese culture, dragons are everywhere and remain important today. Kowloon or "nine dragons" was so named by the last emperor of the Song Dynasty, and the number nine is synonymous with dragons. According to legend, the Yellow Emperor went into battle against nine tribes along the Yellow River Valley. After each victory, he borrowed some aspect of the beaten tribe's totem and incorporated it into his own dragon totem. This is thought to be the reason why Chinese dragons have attributes belonging to nine other creatures. According to folklore, they have eyes like a shrimp, antlers like a deer, jaws like a bull, a nose like a dog, whiskers like a catfish, a lion's mane, a slender tail like a snake, scales like a fish, and claws like a hawk. This multiple hybrid makes a striking creation that is quite different from the traditional Western image.

The abodes of ancient emperors were full of dragon statues and images, which could be seen peering from pillars, adorning ceilings, and curled protectively over roofs. Furniture displayed dragon motifs and carvings. The emperors' robes were called "dragon robes" and their chairs were "dragon chairs." Everything was infused with dragon power, because it was seen as supremely divine. Royal sons were even called "seeds of the dragon" to indicate their status and strength.

THE NINE DRAGONS IN CHINESE MYTHOLOGY

Chinese dragons are the ultimate good fortune symbol. They represent the life force, or chi, within every human. Unlike Western dragons, they do not breathe fire, but instead have the ability to quench the land with water. Wise and friendly, these dragons are sacred and revered, and while they don't have wings they can still fly high and fast, when required.

The horned dragon, *Jiaolong*

This aquatic dragon could change shape, sometimes appearing as a fish or a crocodile, and even taking human form.

The underground dragon, *Dilong*

This dragon has the power to control geological events on Earth.

The winged dragon, *Yinglong*

The oldest of all Eastern dragons, the winged dragon commands the rain and is sometimes referred to as a rain deity.

The celestial dragon, *Tianlong*

This dragon protects the palaces of the gods.

The spiritual dragon, *Shenlong*

With power over the winds and rains, the spiritual dragon is linked to the elements.

The dragon of hidden treasures, *Fucanglong*

The guardian of great wealth and treasure underground, this dragon has enormous responsibility.

The coiling dragon, *Panlong*

This dragon inhabits the waters.

The yellow dragon, *Huanglong*

This dragon emerged from the River Luo to show the hero and god Fuxi the elements of writing.

Dragon King

This Chinese deity governs the ocean. He can shapeshift into human form, and lives in a crystal palace beneath the sea. The Dragon King also controls the weather and can conjure rainfall.

japanese dragons

Similar to Chinese dragons, but with three claws instead of four or five, these sacred creatures are revered as symbols of hope, nobility, and prosperity, and usually associated with water.

Ryujin is the Japanese god of the sea and a water dragon. He controls the tides with his magical pearls, and has a palace underwater known as Ryuju.

O Goncho is another famous Japanese dragon, white in color. He lives in a deep pool of water by Kyoto and, according to legend, every fifty years turns into a beautiful golden bird with the howl of a wolf. Despite this glorious transformation, the creature's howl is an omen of famine to come.

A more auspicious tale is that of Raitro the dragon. One day a poor peasant was praying for rain so that his crops would grow. Benevolent Buddha answered his prayers with a loud clap of thunder and a sudden downpour of rain to end the drought. When the peasant turned around in wonder, he discovered a beautiful baby boy on the ground. He and his wife were childless, so they adopted the infant and called him Raitro. As the boy grew, his talent for calling the rain was obvious, and his adoptive family became rich and well fed. When Raitro reached the age of 18, it's said that he gave thanks to his parents for all that they had done for him, then transformed into a stunning white dragon and flew away.

legendary dragons

THE IMOOGI

The Korean legend of the Imoogi tells the tale of a human girl who, upon reaching the age of 17, transforms into a powerful sea serpent. It's easy to tell who she is in human form, for she has the birthmark image of a dragon upon her shoulder. The name itself means "great lizard," and the Imoogi has immense strength, a gift bestowed by the Sun God.

ISE BERE

In direct opposition to the Eastern water dragons who nourish the Earth, African dragons are often thought to be responsible for the dry, barren conditions of the land. Ise Bere is one such dragon, living in the mountains of Futa Jallon, part of what is now Guinea. This gigantic creature drank the River Niger dry. King Samba did his best to destroy the creature and fought him for many years, managing only to pierce his scales with arrows. Eventually, fate turned, and he hit Ise Bere in the heart. When the dragon died, the full force of the River Niger was released, and the drought was ended. It's thought even now that the bones of this tremendous beast lie somewhere beneath the waters of this vast river.

THE SELF-RELIANT DRAGON

In Hawaii, it's thought that all dragons are descended from the Mother Goddess Mo-o-inanea. This beautiful deity appears sometimes as a woman, and sometimes as a dragon. She is responsible for distributing her large family of dragons throughout the islands. Two of these, both female, became the guardians of the Pali, at the end of the Nuuanu Valley. As the centuries passed, these dragon women changed into huge standing stones, which were thought to have magical powers. Mo-o-inanea was worshipped by the ancients and known as the "self-reliant dragon."

NIDHOGG, JORMUNGAND, AND FAFNIR

The Norse people have a love-hate relationship with dragons. While they feature in many epic sagas and tales, in which they are usually defeated by the hero, they are also associated with great courage and strength. The wealthiest longships would sail into battle with a dragon head at the bow or stern, and it was common practice for warriors to wave dragon flags in an attempt to scare the opposition. Impressive and imposing, dragons were important to the Vikings and became an integral part of their storytelling.

* **Nidhogg:** In Norse, the name Nidhogg means "malice striker," and it's a fitting title for this fiendish dragon. Nidhogg spends its days gnawing at the roots of Yggdrasil, the world tree, while finding time to torment those souls in Hel, the Nordic version of hell.

* **Jormungand:** This dragon is serpent-like in its appearance. Known as the "great beast," a literal translation of its name, Jormungand is the offspring of the trickster god Loki and the giantess Angrboda. This enormous creature encircles Midgard (Earth) and is the foe of the god of thunder, Thor.

* **Fafnir:** The hero Sigurd slays this terrifying beast, the guardian of immense treasure. Fafnir was the son of the king of the dwarves, but was supposedly cursed by a magic ring and transformed into a hideous dragon.

PART 2

DRAGON
spotting

Dragons exist and they are everywhere, from the very corners of your mind, your dreams and fantasies, to the epic tales they haunt. You'll find them, often without looking— peering from the crinkled pages of books, scales faded by the print, or in a full-on blast of vibrant color found in the realms of fantasy artwork and posters. Billboards cower to them. Canvas contains their secrets in oils. Movies and television shows offer a taste of the reality—but you can still search for more…

here be dragons

You want dragons to be real. You *need* them to be real—
and they are, because they're an archetype and they stir
something primal within the human psyche. You want to see
them first hand, to feel their presence like a true dragon
aficionado. First, though, you must understand the rules, for
dragon spotting is a precarious pastime. So dust yourself down,
take a deep breath, and prepare to meet your dragon!

DOS AND DON'TS

* **Do your homework.** Get to know as much as you can
  about these magnificent creatures. Research the different
  types from around the world, and know their stories.
* **Don't believe the hype.** Dragons get a lot of bad press,
  but the more you read, the more you'll understand why
  this happens, what makes them tick and how precious
  they are.
* **Do surround yourself with dragons.** Fill your home with
  dragon images, pictures, statues, and ornaments. It's a
  universal rule that like attracts like, so by putting out the
  right kind of energy you'll attract more—hence dragons
  attract dragons.
* **Don't lose your sense of humor.** Serious dragon spotters are
  always prepared to look on the lighter side. Have fun in

your explorations of this beast. If you'll let them, dragons will fire your imagination!

* **Do be prepared to look in unusual places.** Dragons have their haunts, like any mythical creature, but they can also be found in locations that you'd least expect. Have an open mind and heart and you're sure to be successful.

DRAGON SPOTTER'S CHECKLIST

Like any good explorer, you need to be prepared. To give you the best chance, and to make the entire experience more pleasurable, you'll need the following:

* **A notebook** in which to make your observations, note down any interesting information that you find, and to draw any dragons that you spot.

* **A bottle of water.** Dragon spotting is thirsty work, and while the water comes in handy for hydration, it's also essential should you stumble on an angry dragon and need to put out a fire fast.

* **Cookies, or your favorite type of sustenance,** preferably something easy to carry. An entire picnic is not a good idea, just in case you should come face to face with a real dragon and need a quick exit. Dragon spotting can be a long and arduous affair, and you will need to keep your energy levels up.

* **Gold.** We're not talking bullion, but some shiny coins and even sparkly stones work a treat to attract this magnificent beast. A word of warning: don't go for cheap imitations. Plastic beads that look like gemstones won't get you anywhere. Dragons are not easily fooled!

* **Your smartphone.** While most mythical creatures avoid modern technology like the plague, dragons are intrigued. They are, after all, highly intelligent and move with the times. They also appreciate anything that makes life easier and more pleasurable.

how to spot a dragon

You could be forgiven for thinking that dragon spotting is an easy pastime. After all, how could you not see a dragon? It's as big as a house, it breathes fire, and it has wings. All telltale clues, you might think, but over the years different types of dragon and mythical beast have evolved, so while you might think it's a dragon, you could just as likely be gazing at a serpent, ouroboros, or wyvern.

Strictly speaking, dragons always have four legs and they breathe fire, although there are variations around the world (see chapter 1 on dragon lore). Most dragons fly, but this doesn't always mean they have wings. Chinese dragons are usually wingless, but they can still maneuver through the air at great speed. If you see something that looks like a dragon, but has two legs, two wings, and a long tail, it's probably a wyvern. These are also much smaller than typical dragons. Serpents are wingless, and resemble giant snakes. An ouroboros is harder to find. It looks something like a serpent or a dragon eating its own tail, so it has a distinctly circular shape.

TOP FIVE DRAGON SPOTTING SITES

* **Castles.** Dragons love castles because they are usually the seat of power, and dragons love power!

* **Caves** are the dwelling of choice for most dragons, giving them privacy, security, and shelter. Unfortunately, dragons are often hunted, so they need somewhere they can hide. Caves are also the ideal place to stash all their treasure—if there's one thing dragons love, it's having a hoard of gold to guard!

* **Remote countryside.** Being dragons, they enjoy taking flight, but this is something they can't do in busy, built-up areas. Wide open spaces are their playground.

* **Islands.** For the same reason that they love remote countryside, dragons will seek out uninhabited islands that allow them the luxury of moving about with freedom.

* **Country houses and gardens.** If you're looking for dragon images, you might get lucky in a stately home—not only in the paintings hanging on the walls, but also in the gardens, where ornate statues often have a dragon theme.

FIVE FAVORITE DRAGON PASTIMES

You know where to find them, and you've done your homework, but in order to give yourself the edge over other dragon spotters, you need to consider their favorite pastimes. Yes, even dragons have hobbies!

★ **Guarding.** While they prefer to guard a treasure trove of sparkling gold and gemstones, they're not fussy. Dragons love to keep watch and use their protective powers for good. Better than a guard dog, although more difficult to house!

★ **Flying.** Another obvious one, but they do enjoy taking to the air, and the higher the better. Keep your eyes peeled during plane journeys and you might just catch sight of a dragon in flight.

★ **Wooing the ladies.** You may be surprised to hear this, but it makes sense. Dragons are known for their charm and have been portrayed as smooth talkers in many popular movies. Folklore suggests that they prefer to devour maidens rather than romance them, but this is an assumption. In reality, when dragons are given a beautiful woman as a sacrifice, it's because they enjoy her company. By the same token, female dragons enjoy the charms of an affable gent.

* **Hide and seek.** A favorite party game for any self-respecting dragon—they get to use their super-secretive hiding skills, and also to show off their hunting prowess as they seek. The only problem is their enormous size, which can give the game away before it's even started!

* **Playing with fire.** This is not a recommended pastime for humans, but dragons are skilled fire operatives (and sometimes pyromaniacs). Bonfires are particularly attractive to dragons.

dragons in fiction

From the Book of Job somewhere deep in the annals of the fifth century, and the sea monster Leviathan, to Drogon, Viserion, and Rhaegal, from George R.R. Martin's infamous *Game of Thrones*, dragons are everywhere in literature. They make the perfect enemy, or savior, depending on the tale, and in some cases even the main protagonist. They don't do things by halves and can add color and depth to any piece of fiction, making them the writer's friend, particularly when the story needs to step up a gear. They can be adversaries, companions, warriors, and leaders. In some stories they're even part human, shifting with ease from one form to another. Dragons are flexible, and as long as they're treated with respect, they will bring adventure and excitement to any narrative.

They appear in works from the Middle Ages, including *Beowulf* and Geoffrey of Monmouth's *Historia Regum Britanniae*, in which dragons can be found lurking in an underground lake. These creatures are terrifying, like the dragon slayed by George in *The Golden Legend*. They are callous and without remorse, and we want the heroes in these tales to be victorious in their capture, but over time opinions in fiction change. Lewis Carroll's famous Jabberwock is another creature with attitude. Known for its "jaws that bite" and "eyes of flame," it's not something any reader would like to cross paths with in reality, but from the safety of the sofa and the pages of the book, it's a form of entertainment. Contemporaries and friends C.S. Lewis and J.R.R. Tolkien had their own take on dragons, portraying their lust for gold as a weakness, although Tolkien's dragons are exceptionally intelligent and often use magic to get their own way.

In the 1960s, Ursula Le Guin began her popular fantasy series *Earthsea*. In these tales the dragon archetype receives a mini makeover and the dragons, which appear throughout, go from treasure-hungry monsters to wise and powerful characters with an air of nobility. These dragons have an almost godly status and share an ancestry with humanity.

In the 1980s, dragons even became humorous, featuring in Terry Pratchett's *Discworld* series. Here you'll find two different types of dragon, one traditional and noble, and the other very different. Known as Swamp Dragons, these latter beasts are the size of a small dog and kept as pets, although their fire-breathing abilities mean they don't tend to last long.

Harry Potter meets his fair share of dragons during his time at Hogwarts. These dragons hark back to their scarier forebears and are considered highly dangerous, if also not particularly clever. More recently, Laurence Yep and Joanne Ryder have produced *A Dragon's Guide to the Care and Feeding of Humans*, which is worth a read if you want to delve into the dragon's mind and see the world from its perspective.

With so many stories to discover, you'll never run out of material. More importantly, the dragon's prominence as a key archetype means that there will always be more narratives written. The dragon's tale is a never-ending story.

dragons in the movies

Fantasy fans will already know that dragons play an integral part in movies of that genre and have done for many years. From the evil predators and villains of the piece to more genteel characters, providing wisdom, friendship, and a helping wing to the hero, dragons always have a role to play.

They bring an element of magic and mystery to any cinematic production, turning the movie theater into a place of great imagination, where you can journey into other worlds. Whether your fancy is for faraway lands and the dry dustiness of desert islands, or you prefer something more modern and urban, magic Harry Potter style, there is something for everyone. From the treasure-hungry avarice of Smaug in *The Hobbit* to the endearing charm of Toothless in the animated epic *How to Train your Dragon*, each has a particular allure, a magnetism that keeps us glued to the screen.

If you're looking for old-school charisma, the beguiling Draco of *Dragonheart* fame will surely win your heart. This honorable old dragon, the last of his kind, exudes a wisdom and understanding that sit well with the Eastern philosophy of these great creatures. Disney's animated *Sleeping Beauty* from 1959 is another classic to harbor a dragon, in the shape of the transformed Maleficent. Complete with horns, this purple creation is impressive if not a little scary to watch.

The 1958 version of *The 7th Voyage of Sinbad* includes an altercation between the Cyclops and an immense fire-breathing dragon, virtually unstoppable even without the effects of Dynamation, an early form of CGI (computer-generated imagery).

Dragons may have changed over the years in the way they're portrayed—with the help of special effects, they can now leap from the screen into our world—but the essence of the creature is still the same. Timeless and tantalizing, we simply cannot take our eyes off them, and why should we? Dragons are there to be appreciated. They exist to take our breath away and set our hearts alight.

dragons in myth and legend

Around the world, dragons shift and change in shape and nature, depending on the country and the myth (see chapter 1 on dragons and lore). Their names may differ, but the power of the beast remains. You'll never be bored, no matter what type of dragon you're looking for; there's always something new to learn. Once you delve into folklore, you'll see that dragons have been used since the beginning of time to illustrate important life lessons and help us make sense of the world, even going some way to explaining the cycles of life, death, and rebirth, and various natural phenomena. With enormous strength and magical dexterity, they have the ability to capture our imagination and help us understand some of life's deeper mysteries.

APEP

Apep, the powerful serpent-like dragon in Egyptian mythology, is cunning and clever. He fights the Sun God Ra every night, so he is the bringer of darkness. In the morning, Ra rises again, riding his chariot of brightness through the night sky. This continuous cycle of battle and rebirth is made possible only by the presence of the beast.

ALKLHA

Similarly, the Russian Alklha is a dragon who lived in the heavenly realms, and is responsible for the movements of the sun and the phases of the moon. Every day he would attempt to eat both the sun and the moon, but the sun was too hot and the moon too icy cold, which meant they were always regurgitated. Eventually, the gods intervened and sliced Alklha in two, leaving his top half in the stars and allowing his bottom half to fall to Earth. This didn't stop Alklha's continuous hunger for the planets, but now when he eats the sun or moon, they fall from his broken body and find a new place in the sky.

AIDO HWEDO

Aido Hwedo is a South African dragon, also known as the Rainbow Serpent. Instrumental in the creation of the world, he carried Mawu-Lisa, the supreme creator deity, in his mouth while she formed the Earth. His tracks became the rivers, and the undulating curves of the Earth reflect his movements as he passed through the universe. When the goddess was finished, Aido Hwedo coiled beneath the world in an attempt to support it and keep everything in place, a job he still carries out today.

APALALA

Apalala, the water dragon in Indian mythology, is another dragon with a lesson to share. Originally, a man named Gangi had the power to tame dragons. When he did so, the crops grew and the villagers paid him a tribute every year. As the years passed, the tributes were forgotten and Gangi grew bitter. He prayed that he would turn into a dragon so that he could bring destruction to the people who now scorned him. When he died, he was reborn as a terrifying water serpent named Apalala. Luckily, Buddha intervened. The dragon's heart was healed and he was converted to Buddhism. This popular tale in Buddhist folklore is often recounted to show the healing power of love.

KINEPEIKWA

The Native Americans used dragons as a way of explaining why things happen on the Earth. The Kinepeikwa is a dragon from Shawnee myth, although, unlike others of the same ilk, this enormous serpent transformed in stages, starting life as a fawn with one blue horn and one red horn. During each stage, it would shed a skin to become something new, until eventually it became Kinepeikwa, the dragon that lives in the lake. Some suggest that this tale goes some way toward explaining the stages we go through as humans growing into adulthood.

meet your dragon guide

Spirit guides come in many forms, from loved ones who have passed over and spiritual gurus who have moved on to the next realm, to angelic guides and animal totems, so it's no surprise that dragons also have their place. Being powerful mystical creatures, and attached to specific elements, they can provide strength and guidance when required. As with any guide, you can learn to communicate with them, and the more you practice the easier it will become.

What to do

First you need to create a sacred space where you can meet your dragon. This should be a quiet spot where you won't be disturbed. Make a circle where you can sit comfortably. You might want to outline it with stones or crystals, or use a mat or pillow. As you have not met your dragon before, you are probably not aware if it is associated with a particular element, so to cover all bases it's a good idea to have objects or items associated with all the elements inside the circle. For example, you might have a candle burning to represent fire, a bowl of water or a shell for water, a stone or a handful of soil for earth, and a feather or windchime to represent air.

When you're ready and have all the items gathered, sit in the circle, close your eyes, and focus on your breathing. Notice the gentle rise and fall of your chest and the slow rhythm of each breath. Make a point of extending your inward breath by an extra count, then do the same as you exhale. Repeat this and then extend both breaths by a further count. Let any thoughts float into and out of your mind, but do not focus on them. Simply let them float through your consciousness until you feel totally relaxed. In your mind, picture the entrance to a cave. It can be any kind of cave, something traditional set high in a mountain, deep underground, or even a beautiful crystal cave. The choice is yours.

Notice a warm light flickering from the inside of this dwelling, beckoning you inside. You might also hear music or a voice, or just get a lovely feeling of safety and acceptance. As you enter the cave, the light gets brighter, until you are bathed in a golden glow. You feel strong, powerful, and completely at ease. At this point, look around and take in your surroundings. The cave will be welcoming and may even be plush with decoration. This is the home of your dragon guide, and you should feel totally comfortable in this space.

When you're ready, ask your dragon guide to make itself known to you. It might appear in a shimmer of light in front of you, or emerge slowly from the depths of the cave. It might speak to you before showing itself, or you may just get a flurry of images in your mind. Your dragon guide will communicate in a way that you understand. If you have any questions for your guide, ask them, or if you prefer, just ask your guide for a message or an insight that will help you in the future. Always give thanks for information given, even if it doesn't make sense. You might want to ask if there is something specific that you can use to call upon your dragon guide or its power, for example a particular type of stone, scent, or color.

Alternatively, your guide may give you a power word or phrase, which will help you to connect at any time.

When you're ready to leave, say farewell to your dragon guide and slowly emerge from the cave. Visualize the golden glow around you like a cloak of protection, then gently open your eyes and give your limbs a shake. It's also a good idea to sip a glass of water to help bring you back into the physical world.

DRAGON TIP

Keep a dragon journal so that you can chart your journeys into the spiritual realm and make a note of anything you can remember. Put in as much detail as possible, including pictures and words that will help you connect with your dragon guide. This journal will be your key to communication, and as you progress, you'll find a pattern developing and be able to see how your dragon speaks to you. This will help you form a deeper understanding of some of the signs and symbols used during your visualizations.

PART 3

DRAGON
magic

Dragons are powerful, and any magical practice related to these amazing creatures is also potent stuff. There are a number of ways to perform dragon magic. You can use simple spells to connect with dragon energy or more specific rituals that include dragon-related ingredients. You can summon more than one dragon at a time; there are no set rules. Like any type of magic, dragon magic is flexible. It's about your personal relationship with this mystical creature and how you want to tap into this well of energy in the spiritual realm.

THE
DRAGON
FIRE WITHIN
LIGHTS
UP MY
WORLD

getting started

Before you begin any spell, you need to cleanse your aura. This is because dragon magic has the power to amplify thoughts or feelings, so it's a good idea to remove any negative energy that might be dragging you down or clouding your judgment. You can do this simply by visualizing yourself standing in a shower of white light. This cleansing energy hits the top of your head and cascades over your body, seeping through the pores to clear away tension and negativity. To increase the power of this ritual, take a bowl of hot water and add either a handful of sage leaves, or two or three drops of sage essential oil. Sage is known for its ability to cleanse and purify. Inhale the fresh aroma and waft it around your body, then say: "I am a vessel of pure light. I am cleansed and prepared to create magical energy."

DRAGON TIP

Give the cleansing process a boost by employing some dragon power. Visualize a gleaming white dragon standing above you. Imagine this sacred being opening its jaws to unleash the shower of light. Feel this uplifting energy wash over you.

elemental energy

It's possible to use spells to call on dragon spirits; these encompass the energy of a type of dragon usually associated with an element—earth, water, air, or fire. Each elemental dragon has a particular area of strength, so that you can tailor the spell to suit your needs.

ELEMENTAL DRAGONS

* **Earth dragons** are great for general protection, grounding, and also for sowing seeds for the future. They can help with new growth in any area.
* **Water dragons** bring an abundance of wealth and can also help with emotional troubles and love requests.
* **Air dragons** can assist with creativity, problem solving, and generally bringing more fun and spontaneity into your life.
* **Fire dragons** are associated with swift action; they're also great for self-confidence, self-expression, and success.

SPELL TO SUMMON A DRAGON

Before beginning this spell, you must decide what type of dragon you'd like to attract. There are four different elements—earth, water, air, and fire—so, depending on the element, you'll need specific ingredients. For an earth dragon, you'll need a clump of soil or a stone; for air, a feather; for fire, a candle; and for water, a cup of fresh water.

What to do

* **Clear a circular space on the floor where you can sit, and place your elemental gift beside you.** Spend a few minutes focusing on your breathing and imagine that you're sitting in a circle of bright light.
* **Next, take the gift in both hands.** If it's a candle, light it; if you've a cup of water, dip your fingers into it. Say: "By the power of this element, dragon, I call you to me. Move into this circle with your energy." Close your eyes, and continue breathing deeply.
* **You should feel a shift in the atmosphere as dragon energy draws close.** When you notice the change, continue to breathe and let any thoughts, feelings, or images come to mind. These are direct communications from the dragon spirit.

* **When you've finished the ritual, remember to thank the dragon for honoring you with its presence.** Open your eyes and spend a few minutes holding the elemental gift. Then, when you're ready, release it back to the universe—blow out the candle, scatter the soil or stone outside, pour the water on a plant, and cast the feather into the wind.

my
creative spirit
SOARS
like a
DRAGON

water dragon wealth spell

Dragons, both Eastern and Western, are associated with abundance, whether that's hoarding their treasures or helping others find prosperity. Dragons are the key to improving your financial situation. You'll need a piece of aquamarine and a picture of a waterfall for this spell, which is best performed near freely flowing water. If possible, find a lake, stream, or river where you won't be disturbed. If not, you can carry out this spell when you are running a bath or shower.

What to do

* **Place the aquamarine on top of the picture** of the waterfall.
* **Open your arms and ask the water dragon to enter your world.** As you do this, picture yourself standing in a waterfall. Every drop of water glitters like a diamond, and you realize

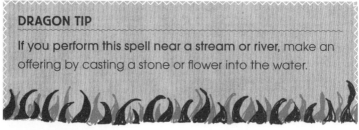

DRAGON TIP

If you perform this spell near a stream or river, make an offering by casting a stone or flower into the water.

that you're standing in a shimmering pool of jewels. Say "thank you" to the water dragon for his abundant gifts.

* **Keep the stone wrapped in the picture close by as a charm to increase your wealth.** You should find that your financial situation improves in dragon-sized leaps and bounds within a few weeks.

my dragon

HEART

gives me

wings

dragon fire success spell

Success is synonymous with dragons. They do not fail in their endeavors, and they can help you reap the rewards you seek. You'll need a red candle and a pin for this spell, along with a red or orange scarf. You can perform it any day, but it's best carried out when the sun is at full strength.

What to do

* **The red candle represents the dragon's fiery breath.** Take the pin and carve a star for success into the wax.
* **Make a circle with the scarf,** and place the candle in the center, ensuring that it's a safe distance from the fabric.
* **Light the candle and gaze into the flame.** Ask the dragon spirits to draw close and bless you with success. If you have a specific project or goal in mind, see yourself achieving it.
* **Let the candle burn down,** then remove the scarf.
* **If you've an important event or meeting and you're hoping for a successful outcome, wear the scarf.** Alternatively, for general success in all things, hang the scarf somewhere near your front door to encourage a steady flow of good fortune into your home.

lucky dragon spell

The Chinese have a long-held belief that dragons are lucky. They bring good fortune and myriad blessings when they enter your life. Tap into this power with a simple spell.

What to do

* There are nine different types of Chinese dragon (see pages 20–21), making nine a symbolic number. Say the following chant nine times, by an open window: "Lucky dragon, hear my plea. Send good fortune now to me." This spell is best performed on a windy day when you can feel the breeze blowing into your home.

DRAGON TIP

To make this spell extra effective, visualize a gold dragon sending a breath of good fortune through your window in the form of a ray of golden light, which floods your home.

dragon love spell

A dragon's heart is a powerful thing, and in tales, it's often the key to its supernatural power. For best results, carry out the spell to summon a dragon first of all. If you want swift results, a fire dragon is your best choice. If you're looking for stability and commitment in a relationship, summon an earth dragon. For romance and to find solutions to love problems, an air dragon is the best option, and if you're seeking a soul mate, go for a water dragon.

What to do

* **Once you've called dragon energy into your space,** take a piece of paper and draw a large heart. Trace around the heart nine times with your finger as you say: "Dragon, amplify my love, bring more love to me. Fill my heart with joy. Dragon, let it be." Repeat this over and over until you've finished tracing around the heart.
* **When you're done,** write any special love requests or wishes in the center of the heart, then place it somewhere safe.
* **Within nine days you should start to notice positive changes in your love life.** After nine weeks those changes will have developed, and after nine months your love request should be fulfilled.

dragon heal my heart ritual

Despite being truly awesome and somewhat feisty, dragons have a softer side. The strength of their power and warmth provides healing energy that can soothe the heart, mind, and soul, and repair emotional damage or trauma.

What to do

* **Find a space where you can lie down and won't be disturbed.** Hold a piece of quartz crystal in both hands and get comfy.
* **Close your eyes and imagine a giant dragon standing above you.** This dragon is here to heal your heart and help you find inner peace and strength. Try to picture the dragon in your mind, to help you connect with its energy. It might appear a certain color or have a distinctive shape.
* **When you're ready,** visualize the dragon sending a stream of fire energy directly to your heart. Feel this fire hit the center of your chest, where your heart chakra is. It fills you with a stream of warmth, which helps to soothe any frayed emotions and steady your breathing. Enjoy the healing sensations as the energy fills your heart and mind.

* **For the best results, repeat this ritual at least once a day for two weeks.** You should find that as the days go on, you feel lighter, calmer, and more positive. Also remember to keep the quartz crystal with you at all times.

DRAGON TIP

For on-the-go healing, hold the quartz crystal over your heart and imagine a fiery dart of dragon's breath entering your heart chakra. Breathe deeply and let this energy settle in your chest.

spell for dragon protection

A dragon's natural urge is to protect, and what better spiritual aid than to have this mighty beast watching over you? You'll need as many images of dragons as you can find. These can be pictures from magazines, posters, or ornaments, or you could have a go at drawing your own. When you apply personal energy by drawing something that is unique to you, you enhance the results of the spell.

What to do

* **Arrange the pictures in a circle around you and sit with your hands resting on your knees in front of you.** Make sure your palms are facing upward in a receiving position.
* **Say:** "Dragon spirits, I call on you. Make me your charge and watch over me, protect me from forces I cannot see."
* **Imagine a circle of dragons gathering around you,** and feel the force of their power and the shade of their enormous wings, shielding you from harm.
* **When you've finished, distribute the pictures and ornaments around your home.** Make sure you have one for every room, and if possible place a picture beneath your entrance mat or by the front door.

I fly with

dragons

every day

dragon guidance ritual

Dragons have been around for centuries and they've seen it all, which makes them incredibly wise to the ways of the world and a great confidante in times of trouble. It's easy to call on dragon guidance. All you have to do is align yourself with dragon power and see the world from their perspective.

What to do

* **If you're dealing with a specific problem,** think of a symbol that sums up the core of the issue. For example, you might have a romantic dilemma, so you might see a heart split in two; or if your problem is related to your home, you might see a small house in your mind.

* **Focus on the symbol you've chosen and imagine it framed in golden light.** Now see it reduce in size until it looks like a pebble on the ground in front of you.

* **Finally, imagine you've wings like a dragon, and picture yourself lifting into the air.** As you fly upward, the symbol, which is already small, becomes more and more distant, until it is a tiny speck that you can hardly see. Say: "Like a dragon, I have perspective. My problems do not own me, I am in control."

* **Repeat this ritual twice a day for three days.** During this time, you should find that you feel better about the issue, and that you can see a way forward. You might receive guidance in the form of a dream, or just an intuitive feeling, but you'll definitely feel more positive and be able to see a number of solutions.

where there is

DARKNESS,

dragon fire

brings

light

spell for psychic assistance

Dragons' eyes, stunning to look at, hold the key to the wisdom
of the world. If you gaze into them, you'll find all the answers
you seek and also insights into the future.

What to do

* **Take a black bowl or cup of water to
  represent the dragon's eye.** Add a
  couple of drops of lavender essential
  oil, and stir with your finger.
* **Place a towel over your head and
  gaze into the bowl.** Breathe deeply
  and let the sweet aroma of the
  lavender relax your mind. If you have
  a specific problem, bring it to your mind; if
  not, simply ask for guidance from your dragon spirit. Ask
  it to speak to you in whatever form it chooses. You might
  see pictures, words, patterns, or something more symbolic.
  The image could appear on the surface of the water, or
  in your head. Either way, it's a psychic message from your
  dragon guide.
* **Make a note of anything you see for future reference.**
  Even if it makes little sense to you now, you may find in the
  coming days that it is relevant in some way.

be a dragon queen ritual

Move over Daenerys "Stormborn," it's your time to shine as the mother of a dragon. This ritual is perfect for when you want to be the best version of yourself, and feel super empowered.

What to do

* **Create a circle of power by picturing a bright sphere of light,** or if you prefer you can mark out the area using stones and crystals.
* **Crouch down in the middle,** with your arms wrapped around your knees. Visualize a pair of dragon wings sprouting from your shoulder blades and stretching outward. You can feel the strength and energy from these wings seeping into the rest of your body.
* **Slowly begin to unfurl,** reaching upward until you're standing tall with your shoulders back and your head tilted to the sky. Cross your arms over your chest, fists clenched firmly and say: "I am dragon. Hear me roar. I am dragon at my core." Then swiftly uncross your arms and stretch them upward, fists still clenched.

DRAGON TIP

Whenever you need a boost during the day, or before any special events or meetings, find a quiet place and repeat the last bit of the ritual, pulling your clenched fists and arms across your chest and repeating the magical mantra out loud. If you can't find a private spot to do this, simply clench your fists and repeat the mantra in your head; it will have the same effect.

firing-on-all-cylinders spell

Think of dragons, and you're likely to picture an impressive
creature, with rippling muscles, gleaming skin, and immense
strength. A dragon in its prime is indestructible and
awesome to behold. You too can give your health
and well-being a much-needed boost with this
dragon spell.

What to do

* **Find a picture of a dragon** and stick it in the center of
  a large piece of plain paper.
* **Next, think about all the words you'd associate with this
  beast.** Choose positive words that indicate strength and
  vitality, such as power, energy, vigor, and force. Write these
  words in red ink around the picture of the dragon.
* **Place a gold coin in the center of the paper,** then close
  your eyes. Let both hands hover palms down above the
  picture, and say: "Dragon energy pours through my body
  and soul. I am strong, centered, and whole." Open your
  eyes, and read the words on the page out loud, then say:
  "These qualities are mine from this moment in time."

* Repeat once a week at the same time for a month, and you should start to see and feel the results. If you want to send dragon healing to someone else, simply refer to that person instead of yourself in the chant.

DRAGON TIP

Between each ritual, keep the coin somewhere on your person as a dragon charm, but be sure not to use or lose it!

create a dragon altar

If you want to tap into dragon energy every day, it's a good idea to create your own dragon altar. This will be a space that you can use to communicate with your dragon guides, tap into their wisdom, and generally feel safe and empowered. Think of it as a type of shrine or sacred space where you can show your appreciation to this marvelous creature. All you need is a small coffee table, shelf, or even a window ledge.

What to do

★ **Start by clearing and cleansing the area.** Take a small bowl of hot water and add a sprig of sage, or a couple of drops of rosemary essential oil. Leave it in this space overnight to purify the energy. Then decorate the altar using all things dragon. Think about colors and textures that you might associate with this resplendent beast, and also the elements of earth, water, air, and fire. You may want to dedicate the space to a specific type of dragon, or even one you've chosen from folklore. If so, think about symbols that are personal to this creature that will help you connect to its power.

* **Include images of dragons plus models, sculptures, and any other related ornaments.** A dragon box is a good idea. You can use it to store any quotations, words, phrases, and dragon spells that are important to you. You might want to set aside some space for your dragon journal, too (see page 47). A candle is an essential addition to any kind of altar, because, once lit, it can create the right kind of atmosphere. A plant or a vase of flowers is also beneficial, encouraging positive energy to grow.

Think of this space as your dragon's lair. It's a place you can come to reboot and recharge after a stressful day. If you are in search of guidance, strength, or wisdom, make the dragon altar your first stop!

PART 4

how to train your own

DRAGON

We all have a dragon inside—not a physical, fire-breathing beast, of course, but a power that we can use in a positive way. Consider those moments in life when you've felt fired up, completely impassioned about something, or even someone! You're on a roll and it feels as though you could achieve anything you set your mind to. Your body bristles with excitement and the knowledge that you can make your dreams come true. You are strong, centered, and in charge of your destiny. This is your inner dragon at work. It's the fire in your belly, a buzz of adrenalin channeled in a productive way. Once you recognize this energy, you can use it to feel more confident and to manifest your dreams.

find your fire

Dragons and fire go hand in hand. You rarely have one without the other, and even if the beast in question doesn't spit flames, its fire comes in the timbre of its courage and spirit. You too can find your fire and use it to boost your personal power by practicing this easy exercise.

What to do

* **Place both hands over your solar plexus,** the area just above your belly button. This is the seat of your intuition, and the place where you're likely to experience the first

---

DRAGON TIP

Think of something that you'd like to achieve. See yourself reaching this goal in your mind, and as you exhale and release the fire, infuse the image with dragon energy. Imagine tendrils of flame wrapping around the picture until it bursts into beautiful bellowing fire!

jitters of excitement when something positive is about to happen, or a tight, heavy sensation when things don't feel right.

* **Close your eyes and breathe deeply.** Hold your breath for a slow count of four, then exhale for a slow count of four. You should feel calm and relaxed. Repeat and imagine a flame growing beneath your hands. You can feel it flickering inside, as it gently twists and extends upward. The flame gets bigger and brighter with every breath you take. You can feel the warmth spreading through your stomach, as the flame grows into a crackling fire, which stretches up through your neck and throat.

* **Take a deep breath in and imagine unleashing that flame through your mouth as you exhale.** Feel the force, as you thrust this powerful energy into the world.

uncover your scales

Dragons have scales to protect them from attack. This magical outer layer of skin is impenetrable and allows them to move with ease while rebuffing negative energy. You can create your own dragon-inspired armor for those occasions when you feel vulnerable.

DRAGON TIP

Visualize your scales in full color to give your protection extra edge, depending on your quest. For financial protection and money matters, go for gleaming green; for matters of the heart, vibrant red or deep pink; to create a psychic defense, opt for a purple hue; and for general all-round strength and protection, sleek and shiny black.

What to do

* **Stand with your feet hip-width apart** and your shoulders relaxed.
* **Turn your attention to the top of your head.** Imagine a thick layer of scales around your skull. Feel it spreading over your body, running down your face and the sides of your neck, covering each arm, your shoulders and spine, and then sliding down each leg, until you're fully encased. The scales are light but impenetrable and a part of your skin. Any negative energy in the form of thoughts or hurtful words or emotions will be repelled, bouncing from the scales without reaching your core.
* **To finish, say:** "My scales repel that which means me harm." Use this technique whenever you need to feel strong and secure.

bare your teeth

A dragon's teeth are ferocious tools, used to rip apart its prey. They act as a warning to those who would dare to challenge or attack. Let's face it, dragons don't back down. They stand their ground and stand up for themselves, and while we might not want to be so aggressive, we can learn something from their assertive behavior.

What to do

* **Make a list of all your positive traits,** using a word for each. You might write such things as "kindness," "passion," "imagination." Consider each word as a dragon's tooth. It is strong and it belongs to you. It makes up your personality and who you are.

* **Repeat the list often in your mind,** so that it remains fresh. Whenever you feel challenged, run through the list of words. These are your tools. This is where your strength lies. Be like a dragon, know who you are, and stand your ground.

DRAGON TIP

Each week, focus on one strength that you've identified. List the number of ways that you show this strength, and make a point of using it more. For example, if you chose "kindness," you might consider a way you can tap into that, perhaps by volunteering, helping a neighbor, or practicing kindness in some other way. If you chose "imagination," you could spend some time thinking creatively this week, whether by writing a poem or painting a picture, or even trying to find new solutions to any problems you may have had recently. By doing this, you're perfecting that strength and making it work. In effect, you're polishing and sharpening your metaphoric teeth!

reveal your roar

Although dragons don't roar in the traditional sense, the noise they make is one way of showing their immense power. You too have the ability to let loose and make your mark on the world.

What to do

* **Start by channeling your voice with a simple chant.** Make sure you feel relaxed, stand tall, and breathe deeply. Then make the sound "ahhhhhh." Let this reverberate through your chest, becoming deeper and more resonate. You should feel a slight vibration in the chest area.
* **With each attempt, get louder.** Imagine you're a dragon releasing its call to the wild. Pour all your power into this sound. Repeat as often as feels right.
* **To finish, say:** "I am dragon. Hear me roar!"

I am dragon,
hear me
ROAR

learn to fly

Dragons are creatures of the air. They fly high and far, and this gives them the edge, because it means they can move fast, cover long distances, and take a dragon's-eye view of the world. You can replicate this feeling of freedom, and cultivate the ability to look at the world from a much wider and more inspiring perspective. For best results, perform the following exercise when you need objectivity, or you have a problem to solve. It will help to clear and open your mind, and you'll be able to see an array of limitless possibilities and options available to you.

What to do

* **Find somewhere comfortable to sit,** breathe deeply, and focus your attention on your surroundings.

* **Now imagine you are getting bigger,** growing taller and wider, seeping out of the space that surrounds you. With each breath, you grow until you're bigger than a house, stretching up into the sky and covering the land. You can see everything below you, and you are connected to everything.

* **Eventually, you stretch so far and wide that you become the sky and can see the earth below.** You can see every plant and tree, every building and person. In that moment, you understand that you have the power to create anything you want in your world. There is no limit to your potential. You can fly with dragons!

* **When you're ready, let yourself return to your body,** to the room that you are sitting in. Breathe deeply and relax.

DRAGON TIP

As you expand your outlook and reach out beyond the four walls, picture yourself sprouting wings. Feel them extending from your shoulders and stretching outward so that you can fly. You can go anywhere in the world, as long as you can picture it in your mind.

dragon breath

If the thought of dragon breath makes you recoil, don't worry. This is an altogether different type of breath that will leave you feeling refreshed and energized. It's universally accepted that dragons breathe fire. That is what makes them so exciting, and scary. It's also one of their superpowers. Learn to breathe like a dragon and you'll feel empowered in any situation. You can also use dragon breathing to help you manifest the things you want. Think of it as cosmic ordering with extra attitude!

What to do

* **Stand with your feet hip-width apart.** Lean forward from the hips and gently lower your torso until your head is almost touching your knees. Let your arms hang loose. Take a deep breath in and unfurl your body, slowly raising yourself into a standing position.

* **Place your hands on your hips and carefully lean back from the waist, then exhale.** As you release the breath, imagine firing it like an arrow into the sky.

* **Repeat three times.** If practiced every morning, this exercise will not only give you an energy boost, but also leave you feeling inspired for the rest of the day.

DRAGON TIP

As you exhale each time, make a statement to the universe about your future hopes and dreams. You might say: "I am happy, prosperous, and fulfilled in all I do," or "I have the perfect life for me, I love and I am loved." Do this every day for a month to see results.

light the spark

Dragon energy can help to fire up your creative spirit, which in turn will make you feel energized, inspired, and motivated. Let's face it, there's nothing more dynamic than a dragon as it rockets through the air. It doesn't matter whether you have a particular talent or not. Tapping into dragon power will help you manifest new opportunities and engage your imagination in lots of ways.

For the following exercise, first invest in a piece of Septarian, also known as Dragon Stone. Composed of calcite and aragonite, this stone has a wonderfully uplifting energy and will imbue you with creative confidence.

What to do

* **Place the stone on your head, in the center of your scalp.** Close your eyes and breathe deeply. Clear your mind and begin to connect with the energy of the Dragon Stone. You should feel a slight tingling

sensation on your scalp, and this will begin to travel down your spine.

* Say the following magical chant: "I ignite my creative spirit, the spark that lives in me. I release my inner dragon, and set this power free." Imagine a burst of flames shooting through the top of your head, exploding into the universe.

* Remove the stone and keep it with you as a charm, either on a chain or in a velvet pouch that you can carry in your pocket or purse.

DRAGON TIP

When you need inspiration, an idea, or a new opportunity, hold the stone in both hands and repeat the magical chant in your head. Ask yourself, "What would my inner dragon do or say?" Then relax and let your creative spirit do the work.

cultivate a dragon heart

Dragons are brave. Their courage is legendary. They are often portrayed as winged fiends in the West, but they do not shy away from a battle. If it's something they believe in, they will see it through come what may. This tenacious spirit, along with their honor, indicates one thing—a courageous and noble heart. You can develop this kind of attitude by giving your heart chakra a much-needed boost of dragon energy.

For the following exercise to work, you must first activate the heart chakra, which is in the center of the chest.

What to do

* **Lie down and make sure you are comfortable.** Place both hands palm down on your chest. Breathe slowly and deeply until you feel relaxed. After a while, you should sense a soft

---

DRAGON TIP

Give this ritual extra oomph by holding a picture of a dragon against your heart chakra as you perform the exercise. When you've finished, keep the picture with you so that whenever you need a boost, you can pull it out and repeat the magical affirmation.

warmth emanating from your chest into your hands.

* **Now imagine a pink rosebud beneath your fingers.** Each time you exhale, the petals unfurl a little more, until the flower is fully open. In the center of the rose, there is a ball of dazzling red light. This is the energy center of your chakra.

* **Picture a friendly dragon spirit standing over you.** He slowly lowers his head until it's hovering above your heart chakra. You can feel waves of loving energy coming from this mythical beast, and you feel strong, relaxed, and balanced. The dragon may speak to you at this point, or simply stare into your eyes and transfer a message or some words of hope and encouragement. Slowly it opens its jaws and sends a stream of fiery energy directly into your heart. You should feel an instant burst of warmth and power as this energy disperses through your system.

* **At this point you might want to make a positive affirmation,** such as, "My heart is infused with dragon power. I am strong and courageous. I stand up for what I believe in, and support what is good, honest, and true."

flex your dragon muscles

Dragons are mighty creatures, with enormous yet flexible muscles and legs that support them when under fire. It's no wonder they know how to stand tall and are such worthy adversaries. Find your perfect power posture and follow suit!

What to do

* **Stand feet hip-width apart and let your weight drop down into your soles.** Bend your knees slightly and bounce gently without lifting your feet off the ground. Enjoy the sensation of being supported by the earth and anchored by your legs.

* **Take a deep breath and stand up tall, stretching your spine and lowering your shoulders.** Let your chin tilt upward a little, and imagine a cord attached to the top of your head, gradually pulling you upward. Imagine two fabulous wings spreading outward from each shoulder blade, helping to centralize your balance.

* **Pay attention to each part of your body in turn.** Notice how it feels. Does the muscle feel tense or relaxed, and can you sense any pain? Bend and straighten your legs, flex your arms, and roll your shoulders forward and back. Turn your neck in both directions and let your head fall forward gently, then return to its normal position. Give your body an all-over MOT so that you are firing on all cylinders.

* **If you notice anything that doesn't feel right,** make a note to do something about it, whether that's in the form of exercise, massage, or getting any aches and pains checked out.

DRAGON TIP

If you're struggling with self-doubt, or a loss of confidence, work on your posture. Spend a few minutes letting your weight fall to your feet, as detailed in the previous exercise. This will help you feel secure and supported. As you do this, repeat the affirmation, "I am dragon, I am strong," several times.

dragon mantras

Using mantras is one of the best ways to unleash your inner dragon. These positive statements help to send a powerful message to your subconscious and promote dragon energy. You can create your own dragon mantras by thinking about the kind of dragon qualities that you would like to adopt, or you can adapt simple mantras to suit your needs. A mantra is unique, so make it personal to you. Ask yourself what dragons mean to you and what they represent in your life. Use this as a starting point. There are several examples of mantras throughout this book, just like the one opposite.

You can have more than one mantra, and you can use it anytime you need a burst of dragon power. Simply repeat the mantra in your mind or out loud, at least twice a day.

To increase the effectiveness of the mantra, it helps if you can visualize a dragon standing behind you, or an image that fits the wording. For example, if you say: "I fly with dragons every day," picture yourself soaring through the sky with a group of dragons. If you say: "The dragon fire within lights up my world," imagine your entire body surrounded by a ring of fire. The more imagination you use, the more powerful and successful the mantra will be.

THINK

BRIGHT

THINK

GLORIOUS

THINK

DRAGON

I AM DRAGON

In all the dark and empty places
That's where dragons be.
A coiled spring beneath the earth
Invisible to see.
All serpentine, a thread of light
with scales of molten black
And eyes that tell a thousand tales
of wishes taken back.
Blazing with an ardor bright
that nothing could endure.
The dragon pushes through the night
when others are not sure.

And should you wish to run and hide

The beast it will not falter

With steely courage at its wing

and honor as its bolster.

A wiser creature, there is none

while dragons walk the earth

Between the spaces, veils, and time

From first breath to rebirth.

And should you wish its presence near

you don't need to look far.

The dragon is within your heart

A part of who you are.

PART 5

be a

DRAGON QUEEN

It's one thing to know all about dragons, but to truly understand their greatness, you need to embrace your inner dragon queen: become at one with the beast, and emulate its glory in any way you can. After all, imitation is a form of flattery, and as you model yourself on these majestic creatures, you'll find it easier to aspire to their admirable qualities. Whether you fancy adding a touch of dragon magic to your nails, styling your hair in the fashion of a warrior queen, or going all-out shimmering serpent with a full face of makeup, the choice is yours!

dragon makeup

If you're looking for a hot new look, you can't go far wrong with some dragon-inspired makeup. It's big, bold, and mesmerizing. Picture a lone dragon glistening in the moonlight, its scales almost catching fire as pinpricks of light reflect a magical glow. Then emulate this with the shades you use. Think shimmering skin tones ranging from pearlescent to burnished gold. Add touches of amber and rosy red if you want to heat things up, or deep ocean blue with glints of emerald green for a water-dragon feel. Eyes must be ultra-dramatic, which means lashings of thick black eyeliner and mascara to accentuate the power of your peepers. This look isn't understated. It's about being center stage, beneath the spotlight, and larger than life. Quite frankly, anything goes, as long as it's bright, feisty, and iridescent.

DRAGON MAKEUP KIT

If you're going for this look, it's a good idea to invest in some beauty essentials.

Primer or moisturizer: It's not always important to wear foundation as a base, particularly if you're going for full-on scales and lots of artwork, but it is crucial to have clean, primed skin. A good primer or moisturizer is the perfect starting point. Go for something non-greasy that balances out your natural skin tone. Moisturizers that are easily absorbed and leave a soft, clear base are ideal.

Pigments: Pigments are a fine, loose powder and the main ingredient in eyeshadow (minus the binder that keeps them pressed in a pan). Mix pigment with a little water to create a color base that can be painted on your face if you're going for a full-on dragon look. Metallic pigments can be particularly effective.

Eyebrow pencils: Depending on the look you want to achieve, you may decide to blot out your eyebrows using foundation or makeup glue (see page 106), but you can create a stunning visage using colored eyebrow pencils. Pick matt shades that match the type of dragon you're going for, so for a water dragon, you might use azure blue or emerald green, but for a fire dragon, red or orange.

Eyeliner: Whether you're into liquid liner or prefer something more matt, it's a good idea to invest in both. Make inky black your go-to color, but also opt for a range of different hues to complement the eyeshadows that you use. Matt eyeliners are best for creating lots of scales on the skin, as they don't smudge or blur. Liquid liners are great if you want to accentuate the eyes, and they make it easy to perfect the feline flick, an essential part of every dragon queen's look.

Eyeshadow: This is your excuse to experiment with color and go for something that you might not normally wear. Dragon makeup is vibrant and bold, so while a pea-green shade might not be your usual choice, it works well alongside emerald hues to give you a serpentine look. Vivid jewel-like hues look particularly fantastic on darker skin—think deep purple and violet, shimmering turquoise, and bright orange. Be radical and have fun. Test colors on your skin and, most importantly, go for shadows with sheen. Think pearlescent, luminous, and super glamorous. Dragons are meant to be seen!

Lipstick: Anything goes with lipstick, but the shades that tend to match most looks are black, purple, violet, and deep blood red, matt or gloss depending just how much attention you want to draw. Dust eyeshadow on your lips to match the rest of your face, if you want the focus fixed firmly on your eyes.

Contact lenses: If you're looking to steal the limelight, wear cat's-eye contacts! This provides a stunning contrast against the dark scales. You can also wear colored lenses to tie in with your look—red gives a fierce glare, while blue or green bring to mind the depths of the ocean.

BASIC TECHNIQUES

To create a perfect, polished look, it's worth practicing a few basic skills that you can apply to any dragon look. This gives you the ideal base from which you can be more inventive.

Hide your eyebrows: In an authentic dragon look, your eyebrows might look a little out of place! To conceal them, you can use a washable nontoxic glue stick. Brush your brows, then apply a layer of glue, let dry, and repeat. Then cover the eyebrow area with concealer or foundation for a smooth base.

Dramatic eyes: For a sassy feline flick using a black gel eyeliner, start in the center of your upper eyelid so that you have a clear view of what you're doing. Draw a line as close to the lashes as you can. From the outer corner of the eye, draw a line angled upward, toward the end of your brow. Then draw backward over this line until you reach the center of your upper eyelid. Make sure you fill in any spaces, and for extra drama, make the flick slightly thicker at the end. If you want even more drama, blend a charcoal-gray shadow over your lower lid, sweeping upward along the eyeline flick.

Creating dragon scales: Scales can be created by drawing curved W shapes or sharper V shapes or diamonds. Keep the patterns small, particularly around the eyes and mouth, as you want to accentuate these features, rather than overshadow them. An eyebrow pencil in the color of your choice will provide a softer look, while eyeliner gives edge and drama. Once you've perfected the scales, shade them in with eyeshadow. Go for pearlescent shades that shimmer and smudge over the edges of each scale. For a lifelike effect, continue drawing scales on the collarbone and

neck, but make them bigger and vary the shape.

(To perfect your dragon scales, try them on the back of your hand first. Take a patch of skin and start by creating the right pattern; then dust over with eyeshadow and accentuate the edges using eyeliner. Once you can do it on your hand, you're ready to be let loose on your face and neck.)

An alternative method of painting scales on your face is to use a fishnet wig cap to create a stencil. Place the cap over your face, holding it in place by using bobby pins (grips) in your hair if necessary. Apply some cream eyeshadow to a makeup sponge and dab it onto your face wherever you want your scales, then remove the cap.

CREATING THE LOOK

You've mastered the basics—now comes the fun bit! Engage your imagination and unleash your inner dragon queen.

Find your inspiration: Seek out pictures of your favorite dragons and use them as your starting point. What kind of color are you most attracted to? You might be a turquoise-green lady, with inky-black scales, or perhaps you're a full-on flames girl with burnt amber and copper tones. Dragons come in all shapes and sizes and they don't do things by halves, so if you pick a shade, be prepared to go the extra mile with lots of vivid color, sparkle, and pattern.

Study the shape of each dragon: What does its skin look like and how do the scales appear? What size is it and what about the shape of the eyes? Think about how you can recreate a similar look using cleverly applied make-up. If you're opting for face scales, go for a small design because this will look more realistic and delicate, and it won't overshadow your other features.

Have a go at sketching the type of look you'd like. The clearer it is in your mind, the closer you'll come to re-creating it. Dragon makeup takes time, energy, and focus, but the results more than make up for that.

Practice makes perfect. Don't expect the look to work on your first attempt unless you're a skilled professional. Dragon makeup is an art form, but it should also be fun. Practice the look you want to achieve and do it in stages. For example, one week, focus on your skin and creating shimmering scales. Once you've perfected this, move on to your eyes and then finally your mouth. Then, when you're ready, you should be able to put the look together with ease.

LOOKS TO TRY

* **Silver Dragon Girl:** silver base, grey scales, silver and black eyes, black lips
* **Water Dragon Warrior:** white base, blue scales, blue eyes, violet lips
* **Shimmering Serpent Goddess:** clear base, black and turquoise scales, light-green eyes, purple lips

dragon hair

Dragon hair falls into two categories—one style literally looks dragon-like and the other is fit for a dragon queen. Both are equally striking, depending on how much effort you put in. It's easier to create the latter if you have long hair, but anything goes for dragon hair as long as it's super colorful, outrageous, and in some way bouffant. Think textured spikes and angular cuts, blow-dried, back-combed beehives in an array of different hues. This look is outrageous, meaning you can experiment and, with the help of styling products, achieve something unique.

If your preference is for something more understated, the dragon-queen look could be for you—gorgeous and ultra-feminine. For this style to succeed, you must channel your inner Daenerys. Think cool, confident, and edgy—beautiful tresses of any shade, long, glossy, kept in order with an array of accessories. Braiding is key for this style—it looks wonderful but also has a purpose, which is to keep the rest of the style in place. This is also a good starting place if you don't feel too confident experimenting with color.

DRAGON WARRIOR

This hairstyle is easy to achieve at home, with practice. You'll need a few hair ties (depending on how long your hair is and how many bumps you want to create) and a hair band or a piece of fabric that you can tie around your forehead. Leather braids or bands fit this look well, but if you want to go for something more feminine, a flowered band would also work.

CREATING THE LOOK

Brush your hair to make sure it's tangle-free, then secure a leather band around your forehead. This will help you create the style and keep it in place. Take equal sections of hair from both sides of your head, but leave some flowing tresses at the back. Wrap each section of hair around the band a couple of times. Weave the remaining hair from each section into the

DRAGON TIP

For a true bohemian feel to the dragon warrior style, invest in a selection of ties, ribbons, and beads that you can attach to your braids at various points. Be creative, and add feathers and jewelry for a unique and sassy look.

loose hair at the back. If your hair is longer than mid-length, you'll have to bring it over your shoulder so that you can see what you're doing, or use a mirror to help. You could secure your hair at the end with a single hair tie, but if you have longer hair, it's nice to use several hair ties to hold the hair in at various places to create the "dragon's tail" effect.

QUEEN OF DRAGONS

Similar to the dragon warrior look, but using delicate plaits and leaving more hair loose, this style is glamorous and commanding but with a carefree feel—perfect for wannabe dragon queens. You really need mid-length to long hair for this look to work properly.

CREATING THE LOOK

Start by blow-drying your hair for a windswept look that gives your locks body. Then take a small section of hair from the front of your head and plait it loosely over the top of your head. Do the same with another small section from the opposite side at the front. Continue to do this as many times as you like. The number of plaits you create is up to you. Take a

hair tie and secure all the plaits together loosely at the back, leaving the rest of your hair hanging in gentle waves.

Finally, spray lightly with hairspray to secure everything in place. If you're feeling adventurous, you can accessorize with leather braids, beads, and/or feathers. Tie them in place at the back of your head where all the plaits meet.

DRAGON TIP

If you're going for a regal appearance, invest in some hair jewelry rather than beads or feathers. Go for something with a strong Celtic design, in pewter or silver so that it stands out. Think headbands, slides, or even a tiara, as long as it isn't too dainty or sparkly.

SPIKY FIRE DRAGON HAIR

If you've got fairly short hair, this could be the style for you. Like any respectable dragon, it's bold and breathtaking, and has plenty of oomph. It helps if you've reasonably thick hair, too, but almost any hair type will work with practice. The look is super spiked, like the claws and scales of the sleekest serpent—think unkempt bed head, but with a wow factor. You're not going for perfection here; this style allows you to experiment with your tousles.

DRAGON TIPS

This look works with any hair color, but for maximum effect brightly dyed hair will give a vibrant edge to the style. You can also use colored hairsprays to give each spike a different hue. Customize the look by leaving a longer section of hair at the back, or mix and match your spikes with sections of longer hair between. Alternatively, if you're feeling brave, give yourself a fiery Mohican by shaving each side of your head and then painting with scales. Follow some of the tips in the makeup section.

CREATING THE LOOK

To give your hair depth and height, start by tipping your head forward and spritzing your hair lightly at the roots with hairspray. Back-combing is the key to this look, and it doesn't have to be uniform, so grab random sections of hair and back-comb from the top down in different directions. This will create the spikiness that you need. To define the ends, add a touch of wax, then give your hair a final spritz with hairspray to keep everything in place.

dragon nails

There are many ways to emulate your favorite mythical beast, from a complete hair and facepaint makeover to small but dazzling changes in the way you accessorize each outfit. Nail art lends itself to the creative challenge, and it's surprisingly easy once you get the hang of it. As with all things dragon, anything goes, so take a deep breath, tap into that inner fire, and be dragon gorgeous!

DRAGON NAIL-ART KIT

Having the right tools is essential, so start by setting up a nail-art kit with the basics.

* **Base coat:** To protect your nails and prevent staining, always apply a base coat first.
* **Colors:** Think fierce, blazing shades—red, blue, and green, or metallics. Even black and white can provide dramatic bases for painted designs.
* **Paintbrushes:** Use fine paintbrushes to create intricate designs.
* **Top coat:** Give your nail art a longer life by applying a top coat to protect your work.

CREATING THE LOOK

There are certain things all dragons have in common: super-smooth scales, an iridescent gleam, and power that shines from within. Combine these things for a stylish and unique design.

Super scales: These can be painted on nails, just as you draw them on your face for dragon makeup—simply paint rows of curved Ws or sharp Vs.

Glittery glitz: Flakes of glitter give a magical look without going full-on dragon, and you can't go wrong, because each nail is individual. Apply an initial base coat, let dry, then apply a coat of your chosen base color. While your second coat is still wet, take a pot of loose-flake iridescent glitter and a brush. Dip the brush in the glitter and sprinkle over the nail. Apply as much or as little as you like. The luminescent flakes change color in the light, giving the appearance of steely scales moving beneath the ocean.

DRAGON TIP

If painting your own designs seems too much, why not try artificial nails that are already patterned? A huge range of bold designs are available.

Marbled effect: This brings to mind the ancient grandeur of legendary dragons. Apply a neutral base color in white or gray and let dry. Put a dab each of two or three colors of nail polish onto a palette—perhaps white, black, and silvery gray, or deep inky blue, rich emerald green, and light sky blue. Use equal amounts and then take a makeup sponge and mix the colors together lightly. Using the sponge, apply the mixed color to each nail by dabbing it gently over the base coat. This should give a marbled effect. Apply a final clear matt top coat.

Striking simplicity: A vibrant colored base with a simple design painted on top can evoke power, like the dragon's power that you've awakened in you. Even a single black line down the center of bright-red nails will get you noticed!

dragon tattoos

Whether you've a hankering to be the next girl with the dragon tattoo, or you fancy demonstrating your connection to this mythical creature in a colorful and daring way, some skin art could be the answer. Tattoos have never been more popular, and there's a growing trend for dragon tattoos. Are you a fan of the strong and regal Celtic dragon, or do you prefer something with an Eastern feel? The options are limitless. Again, think about the symbolism of the particular dragon that you choose—you'll be living with it, so it's important to select a depiction that resonates with you.

The fluid shape of the dragon means that it works on almost any part of the body. Most people opt for a shoulder, back, or arm, but dragons can be any size, and since the passion for bigger, bolder designs is on the rise, other folks choose full-body or back designs. Don't let this put you off if you're after something more discreet—dragon tattoos, like the creatures themselves, are flexible.

A Chinese dragon design is particularly versatile. It can be inked with colorful scales, whiskers, and horns, and

CHINESE MAFIA

Dragon tattoos were once a popular choice of the Chinese Mafia, who used full-body designs to conjure up a sense of power and dominance. Today there is no criminal association, but those who choose to wear the dragon still do take into account the type they choose, and also the colors.

incorporated with other celestial symbols. The number nine, which is auspicious in Chinese mythology, has a clear association with dragons, so it's often included in tattoo artwork. Chinese dragons are sometimes depicted with beards of flames, but, as with all tattoos, the choice of design is down to the individual.

Although Western dragons are associated with greed and fear, they are also seen as a positive symbol, the idea being that someone usually has the strength and intelligence to slay the beast. In most cases, this is a knight or warrior of sorts, someone with enough courage and wisdom to face the dragon and come out on top. When people opt for this type of dragon, it can be a way of saying that they've come through the hard times, battled their demons, and are much stronger and more powerful as a result. Celtic dragons lend themselves to tribal designs, although any type of dragon can be given this look.

CHOOSE CAREFULLY

Before you go ahead, give your tattoo serious thought. Remember, it's extremely difficult to get any kind of inking removed or covered, so you must be sure you've plumped for a design that you love and not chosen on a whim.

* **Spend some time perusing dragon artwork.** Make a note of the different styles. You may see something you like, or you may wish to incorporate various shapes into your design. Experiment with designs on paper and collect pictures and dragon-related imagery that appeals. Have

DRAGON TIP

Why not tell an epic tale through your body art, taking inspiration from dragons in myth and legend? Pick a story you like and create the artwork to go with it. Build a storyboard in your mind and on paper, then think how you can amalgamate the images in a unique and truly dragon-inspired design.

a clear idea in your mind of the kind of thing you're looking for. Have an actual picture to hand as well, to help the tattoo artist and avoid any miscommunication.

* **Research the artist.** Ask for examples of previous work and speak to other customers. A professional artist will be happy to show you their portfolio and spend time talking through your requirements.

* **Consider the location of your dragon tattoo.** Do you want it to be on show a lot, or would you prefer something that you can keep covered and reveal as and when it suits you? If you've never had a tattoo before, also think about the time involved. Body art can be painful and time-consuming, depending on where it's situated. Start small and allow yourself to get used to the process.

* **Have fun!** This is an opportunity to unleash your creativity on the world. Think dragon and engage that inner spark.

dragon gems

Crystals and stones transmit energy, and have a positive effect on the aura, the force field that surrounds the body. Dragons are often associated with certain precious and semi-precious stones, whether they're guarding them or just linked to the stone's specific energy pattern. It makes sense, then, that you can work with stones to connect with dragon power, whether you want to carry them or wear them as an eye-catching accessory. A dragon pendant, bracelet, or pair of earrings can help you tap into the fire within and unleash your personal power, turning heads in the process!

STONES TO CHOOSE FROM

Like stepping stones, any type of gem or stone can be used to help you communicate with the spirit world, but some lend themselves to the process more than others. Also, some specific stones match dragon energy. Here are some top choices to get you started.

Quartz: This crystal amplifies energy, so it's an all-rounder and can be used in most dragon spells. Charge a piece of quartz by breathing onto it while visualizing a flow of positive energy passing through the stone. If you want to use it to connect with dragon energy, picture your dragon guide as you cleanse the crystal, and imagine that you can breathe your thoughts and messages into the stone. Wear it as a dragon charm to promote vitality, strength, and happiness.

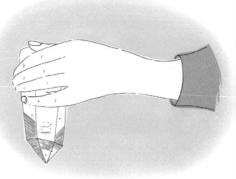

Red jasper: A talisman of warriors, this stone boosts stamina and determination. It can stimulate energy and help you move forward. Associated with wisdom, it's commonly associated with dragons, and often hailed as the "rain bringer." Wear this dynamic stone to help forge a connection with your dragon spirit, and unleash your creative spark on the world.

Garnet: This is a stone of courage, associated with the element of fire. The garnet can be worn or carried for protection. It will help you to connect with your inner dragon, and is a great stone to use in dragon spells that work on manifestation.

Snakeskin agate: The unusual patterns on the surface of this stone can look like a snake's skin, and the stone itself can help you shed your own skin and experience a sense of renewal. Carry or wear it to help boost self-esteem. If you feel an affinity with serpent-like dragons, this is the stone for you.

White opal: Elements of other colors run through this pretty gem, which can help you develop your psychic skills. A great stone to wear when you want to tap into your intuition, it will also help you communicate with your dragon guide. Simply hold it in both hands, close your eyes, and picture your dragon in front of you. Then ask for any advice or guidance.

Pearl: Chinese water dragons are often associated with the pearl, and this gem is thought to have the ability to control the ebb and flow of the tides. Pearls can be carried or worn to balance the emotions, heal the heart, and help you attract water dragons.

dragon whiffs

If you thought smoke and burnt offerings were the only smells associated with these amazing creatures, you'd be wrong. Dragons are magical, and as such have the ability to mesmerize an audience, and not only with their power and prowess. Scent is one of the key ways you can attract attention and leave those you encounter enthralled. Fragrance is often used in spells as a way of raising the right type of energy to match your intent, so if you truly want to exude dragon power, you must choose your perfume wisely.

ESSENTIAL OILS

When mixed with a base oil such as almond or grapeseed, essential oils can be applied to the skin as a scented moisturizer. They have many properties that affect health and well-being, and they also enable you to create your own signature dragon scent that will turn heads and make you feel great from the inside out. Mix and match, taking a couple of drops of each fragrance until you find a combination that suits. The following selection will help to raise your "dragon" vibration, making you feel empowered and full of confidence.

Patchouli: Sultry, sexy, and super sassy, this is the scent of choice if you want to boost your allure, perfect for any would-be dragon princess. This fragrance also increases confidence and personal power, so if you're feeling vulnerable, add it to your armor like an extra set of scales!

Rosemary: Sharp and vibrant, rosemary is the scent of choice if you're looking for clarity and want to keep your senses primed. Wise dragons tune in to their intuition, and rosemary will help you do just that. It also boosts personal power, giving you a strong aura and shielding you from negative energy.

Bergamot: Dynamic and uplifting, this scent will put a spring in your step and boost your happiness quota. It's a warm aroma that any fire dragon would appreciate. Mix with other oils to increase the effect and bring joy to any area of life.

Neroli: Cleansing and inspiring, this gorgeous scent is a breath of fresh air, increasing energy levels and giving your dragon scales a glorious glow. If you've been feeling under the weather, this is the perfect aroma—it will help you to feel balanced and brimming with vitality. It gets the blood flowing, which also helps with motivation, a key aspect of any dragon's personality.

Melissa: As any dragon knows, you need strength, agility, and confidence to navigate the skies and command attention. Melissa can give you this. Bright and bold, this sumptuous scent calms and relieves tension. It alleviates anxiety and bolsters courage, allowing you to face any storm and feed your inner fire.

Juniper: Refreshing and invigorating, juniper-berry oil is the go-to scent when you want to spice things up. It gives an emotional boost and promotes positive thoughts and feelings. Dragons always look on the bright side, and this fragrance will help you do the same, even when the going gets tough.

Orange: Rich and citrusy, this fragrance is good for the soul. A heart healer, it will bring peace and a sense of wholeness. Combine it with other oils to help you feel empowered and to fire up your creative spark.

dragon cocktails

You've got the look, the nails, and even the hair, but to be a true dragon queen you need to experience the power. What better way to assert your authority and affirm your super sassy-status than by treating yourself to a dragon-inspired cocktail? Think glorious fiery hues, and warm, spicy flavor sensations infused with citrus and sprinkled with a dusting of the sweet stuff, to ignite your inner flame. Each of the suggested recipes can be adapted to suit your preference, and there are also some mocktails, should you want to keep a clear head. The choice is yours—after all, you are a dragon queen!

RED DRAGON

The Chinese recognized the power and majesty of the red dragon. Let this lucky symbol change your fortune with each tantalizing sip!

YOU WILL NEED

3 orange slices

2 tsp brown sugar

10 red currants

2 tsp (10ml) fresh lemon juice

2 oz. (60ml) pomegranate liqueur

Champagne, to top up

To garnish: sprig of red currants and half-slices of orange

SERVES 1

Muddle together the orange, sugar, and red currants in a highball glass. Add the lemon juice, pomegranate liqueur, and some crushed ice. Stir. Top up with Champagne, add more ice, and garnish with the red currants and orange slice.

be a dragon queen 133

GREEN DRAGON

The yellowy-green glow of this beauty is like a gleam of sunlight caught in a dragon's scales. Gorgeous to drink, and oh so pretty to look at!

YOU WILL NEED

1 egg white

1¹/₂ oz. (40ml) Calvados

¹/₂ oz. (15ml) yuzu juice

³/₄ oz. (20ml) homemade sugar syrup infused with cucumber peel (see opposite)

1 tsp (5ml) absinthe

1 tsp matcha green-tea powder

A dash of fresh apple juice

To garnish: apple slice with a drop of bitters on it

SERVES 1

Put the egg white in a shaker and stir to break it down. (The egg white gives a silky texture to the cocktail.) Add the rest of the ingredients and ice. Shake, then strain into a glass. Garnish with the slice of apple.

Making the infused sugar syrup

You'll need to prepare the syrup the night before. Mix 2 parts sugar and 1 part water in a pan and heat, stirring, until the sugar is completely dissolved. (If the solution reaches boiling point, do not allow it to boil for long or it will become too thick.) Allow to cool completely. Peel 1 cucumber and put the peel in a sealable container. Add the syrup, stir, allow to steep overnight, then strain.

LIQUID GOLD

Like the languid charms of a dragon's eye, let this cocktail entice you with its fiery magic.

Shake all the ingredients together over ice and strain into a chilled martini glass with a sugared edge.

WATER DRAGON

The gentle kindness of the Chinese Water Dragon is renowned in folklore. This tipple captures the soothing spirit of this divine being.

YOU WILL NEED

2¹/₃ cups (600ml) reposado tequila

³/₄ cup (200ml) blue curaçao

³/₄ cup (200ml) triple sec

1²/₃ cups (400ml) fresh lime juice (about 13 limes)

SERVES 10

Add all the ingredients to a pitcher filled with crushed ice. Stir gently to mix and serve in punch cups or glasses.

DRAGON'S BLOOD

Although this brew is called Dragon's Blood, be reassured that not one single dragon was hurt in the making of it!

YOU WILL NEED

1 oz. (30ml) crème de cassis (black currant-flavored liqueur)

2 oz. (60ml) rose syrup, such as Monin

1 oz. (30ml) fresh lemon juice

clear sparkling lemonade, to top up

ice cubes, to serve

SERVES 1

Half-fill a tumbler with ice. Add the cassis, rose syrup, and lemon juice.

Top up with lemonade and stir gently before serving.

QUEEN OF THE DRAGONS

This juicy mocktail packs a powerful punch. It's the drink of choice for all dragon queens: delicious, invigorating, and a joy to behold!

YOU WILL NEED

2 pints (250g) mixed fresh berries, such as strawberries, raspberries, and blueberries

1 orange, sliced

2 quarts (2 liters) cranberry juice

1 small cucumber, peeled, seeded, and sliced

sparkling water or clear sparkling lemonade, to top up

ice cubes, to serve

SERVES 1

Put the berries, orange slices, and cranberry juice in a large pitcher and chill for 1 hour. When ready to serve, add the cucumber and some ice and top up with sparkling water. Pour into tall glasses or tumblers to serve.

DRAGON'S FIRE

This fruity blend has the power to ignite your inner flame. Enjoy it while imagining yourself bathed in the protective warmth of dragon fire.

YOU WILL NEED

1 cup (100g) frozen mixed berries, thawed

1 tbsp confectioners' (icing) sugar

1 large mango, peeled and pitted (about 9 oz./250g flesh)

1 passion fruit, halved

sparkling water, to top up

ice cubes, to serve

SERVES 2

Put the berries in a bowl and stir in the confectioners' (icing) sugar, mashing well with a fork. Set aside for 15 minutes, then pass through a fine strainer (sieve). Purée the mango flesh in a blender or liquidizer until smooth and stir in the passion-fruit pulp. Put a few ice cubes into 2 tall glasses, add the berry mixture and mango and passion-fruit purée, and top up with sparkling water to serve.

final word

I've tried to cover all things dragon in this book, and to give a balanced view of these beautiful beings that have captivated humankind for centuries. You may love the way they look and want to emulate them, or be a fan of the countless stories that feature them, real or imagined. Perhaps a little dragon magic is something you'd like to dabble in. It doesn't matter how you feel their fiery influence in your life; the important thing is that it's there. Dragons can be whatever you want them to be. They can guide and empower you to follow your dreams, and your heart. When you need a helping hand, protection, or just some rays of sunshine, dragons will provide, if you'll let them. So when life gets you down—and also in those moments when it lifts you up—remember there is only one thing to say, with feeling: **"I AM DRAGON!"**

A DRAGON'S CREED

A Dragon's word is ALWAYS sacred.

When she speaks, she talks to your soul.

When she sees, she looks beyond time to the past before you were born and to a future you can only dream of.

Her eyes hold the wisdom of the world, and if you let it, her gaze will burn a path to your heart, igniting the spark within.

The Dragon does not need to be told anything.

She knows and understands who you really are and what you're made of, and what you really need, and how to achieve it.

When she flies, she soars.

There is no barrier, no limit to what she can do or where she ventures.

She just is.

Protective, strong, and ever present.

Old magic seeps from her scales, and every breath she takes is wrapped up in wonder.

She answers to no one except herself.

She is honor.

She is truth.

And most important of all—she is real.

RECIPE CREDITS

Pages 133–135: William Yeoward
Page 136: Fran Warde
Page 137: Ben Reed
Pages 138–140: Louise Pickford

PHOTOGRAPHY CREDITS

Key: *ph* = photographer

Page 18: Getty Images/© CactuSoup
Pages 40–41, 42–43, 98–99, and 142–143: Dreamstime/© Alexstar
Pages 50 and 110: Getty Images/© St Lowitsch/EyeEm
Page 55: © Ryland Peters and Small/*ph* Steve Painter
Page 58: Getty Images/© Cinoby
Page 65: © Ryland Peters and Small/*ph* Chris Tubbs
Page 68: Getty Images/© Nic_Taylor
Page 85: Getty Images/© Nadine Berghausen/EyeEm
Pages 91 and 126–128: © CICO Books/*ph* Roy Palmer
Page 97: Getty Images/© Adrienne Bresnahan
Page 103: Dreamstime/© Vagengeym
Page 107: Getty Images/© Elizabeth Fernandez
Page 113: Shutterstock/© Alter-ego
Page 115: Shutterstock/© Mila Supinskaya Glashchenko
Page 117: Getty Images/© Casarsa
Page 119: Getty Images/© Mo Baig
Page 120: Dreamstime/© Irina Grigorian
Page 121: Dreamstime/© Elena1110
Page 122: Dreamstime/© Kateryna Alferova
Page 125: Shutterstock/© Salim October
Pages 133–134: © CICO Books/*ph* Gavin Kingcome
Page 136: © Ryland Peters and Small/*ph* Debi Treloar
Pages 137–140: © Ryland Peters and Small/*ph* William Lingwood